T0197620

SPIRITS
OF THE
UNKNOWN

Peggy Lundgren

AuthorHouse™
1663 Liberty Drive
Bloomington, IN 47403
www.authorhouse.com
Phone: 833-262-8899

Because of the dynamic nature of the Internet, any web addresses or links contained in this book may have changed since publication and may no longer be valid. The views expressed in this work are solely those of the author and do not necessarily reflect the views of the publisher, and the publisher hereby disclaims any responsibility for them.

Any people depicted in stock imagery provided by Getty Images are models, and such images are being used for illustrative purposes only.
Certain stock imagery © Getty Images.

This book is printed on acid-free paper.

ISBN: 978-1-7283-2809-6 (sc)
ISBN: 978-1-7283-2808-9 (e)

Library of Congress Control Number: 2019914493

Print information available on the last page.

Published by AuthorHouse 01/13/2021

authorHOUSE·

Hi, I'm Peggy Lundgren, I have been feeling and hearing things that I can see or explain since I was a child. Later, I blocked it out. When I got married, it started back up. My husband also hears and senses things. 40+ years and it is getting stronger. More things are being explained as more questions arise. This book is dedicated to all those that encourage me to do this.

I also enjoy walking by water with my husband and two little dogs. I love being with my daughter. I enjoy talking pictures and great granddaughter. I enjoy taking pictures and I also enjoy meditating. And I also enjoy watching the hawks in the sky.

Enjoy by Peggy Lundgren

The Hanging Tree Monument was put up in 1935, Spokane County, WA.
7 native Americans were hanged there in 1858

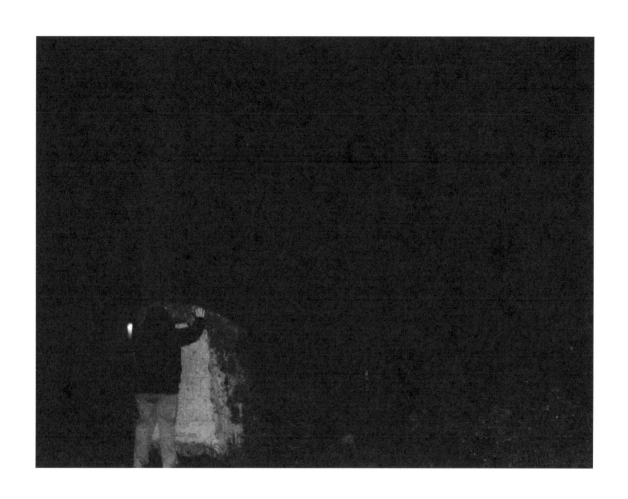

Taken at the monument in Spokane County, WA. It was where the hanging tree was. Orbs were all around me and one tried to land on my shoulder.

John Shields Park, orbs on the trail (daytime)

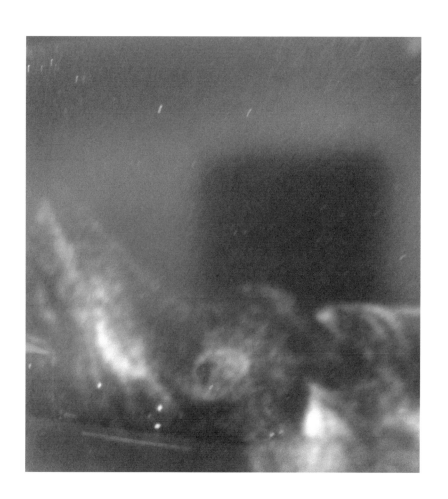

Ghost Dog in our front yard, Spokane. We showed this picture to a neighbor and she said it was similar to a dog that had lived in the area several years before.

Childs face in orb, things forming in the back.

John Shields Park, Spokane. Orbs are moving upwards (note tails on orb) with mist forming.

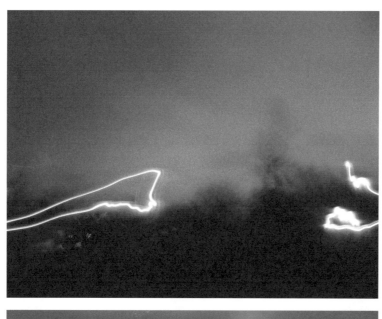

Kris and Aaron on a rock at John Shields Park. The rock was used in
the past for ceremonies by native Americans.

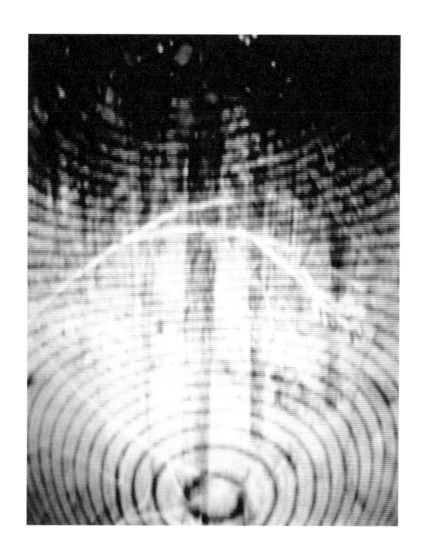

I took several pictures of Kris and Aaron without changing position, but they disappeared in three of the pictures and the background changed.

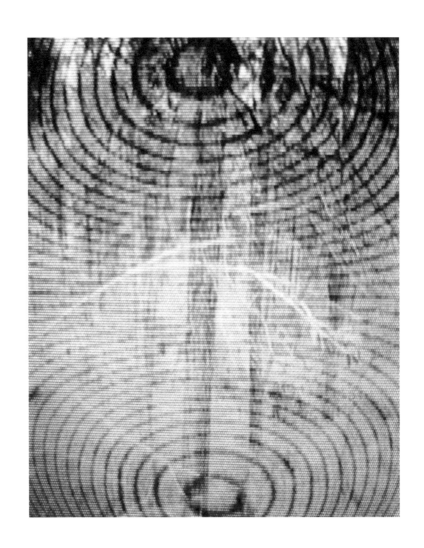

In one of the series of pictures, an object appeared. We blew up the image and it appeared to be a box-type shape with pipe like things attached to it.

In the last picture I took, Kris and Aaron showed up again.

Kris wanted a picture of a rock formation. Note mist figures (one appears to have an old farmers clothes) and someone beside him.

Faces in the mist.

Printed in the United States
By Bookmasters